SIMPLY SCIENCE

# Winter

## by Darlene R. Stille

Content Advisers: Terrence E. Young Jr., M.Ed., M.L.S.,
Jefferson Parish (La.) Public Schools, and Janann Jenner, Ph.D.

Reading Adviser: Dr. Linda D. Labbo,
Department of Reading Education, College of Education,
The University of Georgia

 COMPASS POINT BOOKS

Minneapolis, Minnesota

Compass Point Books
3722 West 50th Street, #115
Minneapolis, MN 55410

Visit Compass Point Books on the Internet at *www.compasspointbooks.com* or e-mail your
request to *custserv@compasspointbooks.com*

Editors: E. Russell Primm, Emily J. Dolbear, and Melissa Stewart
Photo Researcher: Svetlana Zhurkina
Photo Selector: Matthew Eisentrager-Warner
Designer: Bradfordesign, Inc.

**Library of Congress Cataloging-in-Publication Data**

Stille, Darlene R.
    Winter / by Darlene Stille.
      p. cm. — (Simply science)
    Includes bibliographical references and index.
    ISBN 0-7565-0096-6 (hardcover : lib. bdg.)
      1. Winter—Juvenile literature. [1. Winter.] I. Title. II. Simply science (Minneapolis, Minn.)
    QB637.8 .S75 2001
    508.2 —dc21                                                          00-011006

# Table of Contents

**Winter Is Here** . . . . . . . . . . . . . . . . . . . . . . . . . 5

**Freezing and Melting** . . . . . . . . . . . . . . . . . 9

**What Causes Winter** . . . . . . . . . . . . . . 13

**When Winter Comes** . . . . . . . . . . . . . 17

**Life in Winter** . . . . . . . . . . . . . . . . . . . . . 19

**Always Winter** . . . . . . . . . . . . . . . . . . . . 25

**How Winter Ends** . . . . . . . . . . . . . . . . 29

**Glossary** . . . . . . . . . . . . . . . . . . . . . . . . . . 30

**Did You Know?** . . . . . . . . . . . . . . . . . . . 30

**Want to Know More?** . . . . . . . . . . . . 31

**Index** . . . . . . . . . . . . . . . . . . . . . . . . . . . . . 32

## Winter Is Here

Winter is the time of year when you can ride a sled down a hill covered with snow. You can build a snow fort. You can even build a snowman.

Snow is made up of many beautiful **snowflakes**. And every one has a different shape. Snow-flakes are made of tiny pieces of ice called crystals.

Snowflakes come from clouds in the

◀ *Winter in Colorado*

*Winter can be a great* ▶
*time for playing outdoors.*

sky, like raindrops. Snow and rain are both forms of water. When it's warm, we get rain. When it's cold, we get snow.

In most parts of North America, winter weather brings snow. When you go outside to play in the snow, you need a heavy coat, a hat, a scarf, and mittens. They help you stay warm.

If you live in Florida or southern California, you probably

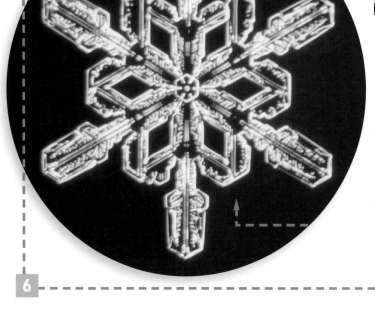

*Snowflakes are made of crystals.*

*It is important to wear lots of clothing to keep warm in winter.*

don't see much snow. But winter in these areas is still cooler than summer. In most parts of the world, winter is the coldest season of the year.

# Freezing and Melting

When you walk outdoors on a cold winter day, you have to be careful. There may be ice on the ground. You could slip and fall. But you can also have fun with ice. You can slide on it and skate on it.

Do you know what ice is? Ice is solid water! You can make ice by putting water in the freezer at home. Water changes into ice when it gets cold enough. This is called

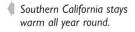

*Southern California stays warm all year round.*

*Icicles on a pine tree* ▶

**freezing**. The same thing happens out-doors. Water on the ground turns to ice when it gets very cold.

Ice turns back into water when it gets warm enough. Take an ice cube out of your freezer and put it in a cup. Watch what happens as the ice gets warm. It turns into water again. This is called **melting**. Outdoors, melting ice makes puddles of water.

Water freezes to become ice. Ice melts to become water. Ice and water are the same thing.

Melting ice

During the winter, water outdoors freezes to make ice.

## What Causes Winter

Have you ever wondered why the seasons change? They change because Earth is always moving. Every year, Earth makes one trip around the sun. And while it moves around the sun, Earth also spins like a top.

To see how Earth moves, roll a piece of clay into a ball. Push a pencil through the center of the clay ball. If you look at a globe, you will see that Earth is shaped like your clay ball. Of course, there is no giant pencil sticking through the Earth. But scientists pretend that there is a large imaginary stick in the middle of Earth.

◀ *Winter snow*

The top of that imaginary stick is called the North Pole. The bottom of the stick is called the South Pole. The stick is called Earth's **axis**. Earth spins around its axis.

Earth's axis is always tipped, or tilted, to one side. So some part of Earth is always tipped away from the sun. Sometimes the north, or top, part of Earth is tipped away from the sun. Sometimes the south, or bottom, part of Earth is tipped away from the sun. It is winter in the part of Earth that is tipped away from the sun.

*Seasons occur as Earth* ▶
*travels around the sun.*

Winter

Fall

Spring

Summer

## When Winter Comes

The north part of Earth is called the **Northern Hemisphere**. It includes North America, Europe, Asia, and part of Africa. In the Northern Hemisphere, winter starts around December 21 and lasts until around March 21. The south part of Earth is called the

Winter in North America begins at the end of December.

Falling temperatures mean winter is near.

**Southern Hemisphere.** When the Northern Hemisphere is tipped away from the sun, the Southern Hemisphere is tipped toward the sun. So when it is winter in the north part of Earth, it is summer in the south part. In the Southern Hemisphere, winter starts around June 21 and ends around September 21.

While it's winter in the Northern Hemisphere, it's summertime in the Southern Hemisphere.

In the winter, squirrels eat food they have stored during the fall.

## Life in Winter

When the ground is covered with snow, many animals have trouble finding food. That's why these animals get ready for winter during summer and fall.

Squirrels gather food and store it for the winter. Snakes, frogs, and some

other animals eat extra food and build up a layer of fat in their bodies.

During the winter, some animals sleep most of the time. Bears make cozy winter dens in caves or curl up in holes in the ground. They get the energy they need to survive from the fat stored in their bodies.

Some birds and **mammals** stay active during the winter. Birds look for seeds left on trees and bushes. They eat seeds

*Snow-covered fir trees*

*A black bear in winter* ▶

you put in a bird feeder. Wolves eat deer and other animals.

Most trees lose their leaves in winter. But some trees stay green all year long. These trees are called **evergreens**. Most evergreen trees do not have leaves. Instead, they have needles. Pine trees, fir trees, and spruce trees are evergreens.

Evergreens have needles instead of leaves.

A forest of evergreen trees

## Always Winter

Some places on Earth have ice and snow on the ground all year long. These places are very cold. The North Pole and the South Pole are the coldest places on Earth. Only special kinds of animals can live in places where it is always cold.

Polar bears live near the North Pole. These huge white bears have thick fur that keeps them

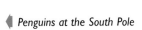
Penguins at the South Pole

The North Pole stays cold year round.

warm and dry. Polar bears eat seals, fish, and other animals.

Some kinds of penguins live near the South Pole. Penguins are black-and-white birds. Penguins do not fly. They waddle along on the ice. Penguins are very good swimmers. They stay dry and warm because they have waterproof feathers. They eat fish and other animals that live in the cold water.

Penguins are suited for cold climates.

Polar bears ▶

## How Winter Ends

The first day of winter is the shortest day of the year. Nightime is longer than daytime. Then daytime starts to last a little longer. The sun sets later and later.

Soon the days begin to grow warmer. You can take off your hat and mittens. Soon you will begin to see the first signs of spring.

*Winter is ending when daylight lasts longer.*

*Warmer days melt the ice formed during the winter.*

# Glossary

**axis**—an imaginary stick running through the center of Earth from the North Pole to the South Pole

**evergreens**—trees or bushes that have needles instead of leaves and stay green all year long

**freezing**—changing from a liquid to a solid

**mammal**—warm-blooded animals with a backbone. They also have hair or fur and feed their young with mother's milk.

**melting**—changing from a solid to a liquid

**Northern Hemisphere**—the half of Earth that is above, or north of, the equator

**snowflakes**—collections of ice crystals that fall from clouds when the weather is cold

**Southern Hemisphere**—the half of Earth that is below, or south of, the equator

# Did You Know?

• Frogs and turtles hibernate during the winter. Sometimes the pond or lake they live in freezes solid. This does not hurt the animals.

• All snowflakes are hexagonal, which means they have six sides. But no two snowflakes are exactly the same.

• Water is a liquid. When water freezes, it forms a solid called ice. When water boils, it forms a gas called steam.

• In winter, the air temperature may not be the best way to measure how cold it is. You also need to think about the wind. The wind chill is lower than the air temperature. That can be very dangerous.

# Want to Know More?

## At the Library

Bancroft, Henrietta, Richard G. Van Gelder, and Helen K. Davie (illustrator). *Animals in Winter*. New York: HarperCollins Juvenile Books, 1997.

Sipiera, Paul P., and Diane M Sipiera. *Seasons*. Danbury, Conn.: Children's Press, 1998.

Supraner, Robyn. *I Can Read about Seasons*. Mahwah, N.J.: Troll, 1999.

## On the Web

**Snowtastic Snow**

*http://tqjunior.thinkquest.org/3876/*

For information about snow and ice and fun things to do during the winter

**Winter Weatherlore and Folklore Forecasts**

*http://www.stormfax.com/wxlore.htm*

For fun ideas about the relationship between summer and winter weather

## Through the Mail

**Farmers' Almanac Order Desk**

P.O. Box 1609

Mount Hope Avenue

Lewiston, ME 04241

To order a seasonal guide with long-range weather forecasts

## On the Road

**Glacier National Park**

P.O. Box 128

West Glacier, MT 59936

406/888-7800

To visit a park with winter weather all year round and 700 miles (1,127 kilometers) of hiking trails

# Index

animals, 19, 21

axis, 14, 30

bears, 21, 25–26

birds, 21, 22, 26

clouds, 5–6

crystals, 5

daytime, 29

evergreens, 22, 30

freezing, 10, 30

globes, 13

ice, 9–10

mammals, 21, 30

melting, 10, 30

North Pole, 14, 25

Northern Hemisphere, 17, 30

penguins, 26

polar bears, 25–26

rain, 6

seasons, 13

snow, 5–6, 8

snowflakes, 5, 30

South Pole, 14, 25

Southern Hemisphere, 18, 30

squirrels, 19

tilt, 14

trees, 22

water, 9–10

## About the Author

Darlene R. Stille is a science editor and writer. She has lived in Chicago, Illinois, all her life. When she was in high school, she fell in love with science. While attending the University of Illinois, she discovered that she also enjoyed writing. Today she feels fortunate to have a career that allows her to pursue both her interests. Darlene R. Stille has written more than thirty books for young people.